HOLY SILENCE REVEALS TRUTH

Bahareh Amidi

Holy
Silence
Reveals
Truth

Bahareh

Copyright © 2022 Bahareh Amidi. All Rights Reserved.

ISBN 978-0-9974573-5-3

cover and interior illustrations by
   Anastasia Lysenko

email: connect@bahareh.com
facebook.com/Bahareh.Amidi
twitter.com/BaharehAmidi
youtube.com/baharehLIVE
instagram.com/bahareh_poetess
www.Bahareh.com

Listen to Holy Silence Reveals Truth

Life is seeing the colors of the rainbow even if your life has been dealt to you in black and white.

The conductor arrives
The strings already tuned
The bows ready to receive the vibrations
The melody the mood, as if the gentle arrival of spring
Each pansy finding its way through the snow
The birds in search of seeds not yet to be found
Could this be the spring of the universe
Could it be the spring of my life
The bulbs ready to break through the earth to arrive
The sounds of the arrival of the bride and groom
    from honeymoon that has consummated
    beauty and truth
The conductor uses his magic wand
Winter gone
Spring arrive

Now somehow the mood is heavy and somber
In the woods a lone home
The smoke coming from the fireplace
Otherwise, no sign of life for centuries around
The sound of the wood burning can almost be heard
    if someone was around
The ants, the mice scurrying around
No signals from the smoke
No smoke in the no signals
Just a wish, a desire
The passerby stops for a while
Stops, listens, then bows
Arrive
Arrive within

Now I've not stopped listening
    but I've started looking at the profiles of
    the people around
Each carrying their own nose their own eyes
    their own identity
Their own hopes and dreams and their own grievances
All
So much carried in a profile, in a note, in a symphony

The small droplets of rain one after the other after that
No race but just joyous symphony of arrivals
    one after the other
As if a whole village of butterflies
    find their way out of the chrysalis and into flight
The rapid flight all in unison
And then arrival in the meadow covered with
    yellow daffodils
The rain, the butterflies, the flowers, the source of All

All

All connected

All encompassed

All arrival is in time

Such eloquence in such huge acceptance

Each and every life is divine

Each and every life is connected to the next

The fog, the mist, the morning dew

All from the same source

A recognition of that space within is welcomed by all

The laced formations of the spider's web waiting for a drop of water or a fly

This is all flight

The tracking of the universe as earth goes
    around the sun patiently
    for 365 days, 52 weeks, 7 days a week, 24 hours a day
    and 60 minutes an hour
    the seconds accumulate waiting
    until each person arrives to their own here and now
I patiently sit to arrive
I wonder at the delicacies of life
The bees buzzing
The spider webbing
The tiger roaring
The snail crawling
All creatures with their own beauty

The camel never complains about his humps
    nor does he compare his short neck
    to that of a giraffe with no hump
    but plenty of spots
You see the lady bug has her own spots and
    the bee his own stripes
I wonder then why oh why humans compare
    their noses, their bumps
    and the creases here and there to those of other humans
Why oh why can't we accept our own bumps,
    spots, and creases
All simply a sign of the Divine

The Divine simply flows when all those in a family,
    in a clan, in a village
    in a country in a universe all accept each other
    and but of course first and foremost accept oneself
Eyes come in different colours and shapes but as long
    as they see they bring forth the light of the Divine-
    and even if they don't see
    they seek the light from within and start seeing
    all that's divine

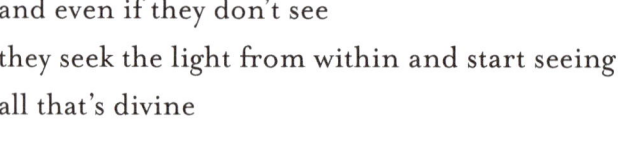

The Divine is not held in one's wallet nor
    in one's credentials
This divinity is simply in the heart
Not to be kept but to be radiated out to the world
    with each breath one can make the world brighter
The path will shine for all those on this same
    carousel of life
This divine exists in the slums where people
    have not a piece of bread
    but also in any mansion full of food but empty of love
There must simply be a thread of divine

With belief Divine is constantly at play
One's awareness becomes higher
    the more connected one gets to the ants crawling around
To get away from one's self, one's own identity then
    the true identity will shine
Shed each layer of skin
Leave behind the masks
Come barefoot
Come with your own self; remembering always
    there is No self
Simply the Divine
The rainbow never arrives with an
    announcement from before
The mysterious play of colours appears in the sky
    as if out of nowhere but in reality in response
    to all the circumstances of the hours, days, weeks before
The temperature, the rain, the fall
This arrival of the rainbow therefore is
    the simplest way to describe
    the connections that bring all existence to life
    under one umbrella
The DIVINE

www.ingramcontent.com/pod-product-compliance
Lightning Source LLC
Chambersburg PA
CBHW040752020526
44118CB00042B/2929